[

Animals with Jobs

Police Dogs

Judith Janda Presnall

KidHaven Press, an imprint of Gale Group, Inc.
10911 Technology Place, San Diego, CA 92127

On cover: A trooper and his dog search for explosives, Logan Airport, Boston.

For all K-9 teams.

Acknowledgments

I appreciate the efforts of Officer Andy Jimenez and Officer Rick Morton, who reviewed my manuscript for accuracy. Officer Jimenez, of the Anaheim (California) Police Department, is a K-9 team trainer and owner/instructor of Falco K9 Academy. Officer Jimenez allowed me and my husband, Lance, to observe and photograph a class training session of five K-9s and their officer handlers. In addition, he answered my numerous questions.

I also shared an evening "ride-along" with Officer Rick Morton of the Simi Valley (California) Police Department and his K-9 Rex. During that time, Rex demonstrated his ability to locate a hidden narcotic.

I am always thankful to Lance, who graciously gives his time and energy taking photos on my various projects, this time at the K-9 training session in Anaheim.

Library of Congress Cataloging-in-Publication Data
Presnall, Judith Janda.
    Police dogs / by Judith Janda Presnall.
      p. cm. — (Animals with jobs)
    Includes bibliographical references and index.
    Summary: Profiles police and detector dogs, their training and abilities, their assets as crime fighters, their partnership with their officer-handlers, and their off-duty activities.
    ISBN 0-7377-0631-7 (acid-free)
    1. Police dogs—Juvenile literature. [1. Police dogs. 2. Dogs.]
    I. Title. II. Series.
    HV8025 .P74 2002
    363.2'32—dc21

00-012814

Contents

Chapter One

The Work of the Police Dog

Dogs do many different jobs for law enforcement. Most patrol with police officers, **searching** for crime **suspects** and missing people, or sniffing out hidden, illegal **drugs**. Some dogs look for hidden bombs or **explosives** in places such as schools, airports, office buildings, and meeting halls.

The specially trained dogs who do this work are called K-9s. *K-9* is short for *canine*, a term used for all members of the dog family. In North America today, over three thousand K-9 programs use nearly thirty thousand police-trained dogs. These dogs have proven their value to law enforcement agencies and their human partners many, many times.

On Patrol

Patrol is the primary duty of many police dogs. The dog rides with a partner (sometimes called a handler) in a patrol car, and when the officer responds to a call, the dog accompanies the officer. Many of these calls are

K-9 Riker is ready for action.

routine. Officers and their K-9 partners are often called to calm unruly parties, help with crowd control, break up fights, and assist other officers at crime scenes.

Sometimes those calls turn out to be anything but routine. Office Andy Jimenez of Anaheim, California, describes one such call. He and Falco, his four-year-old German shepherd police dog, were called out to check on an assault with a deadly weapon at a house. As they walked into the garage, Falco growled. From Falco's growling, Officer Jimenez knew immediately that someone was hiding behind the door leading from the garage to the house. "If Falco would not have alerted me, I would have entered the room and been shot by the suspect, who had earlier shot someone else,"[1] Officer Jimenez says.

Tracking

The keen sense of smell that alerted Falco to a hidden person also helps dogs excel at **tracking** crime suspects and missing people. Tracking involves following a scent either from clothing or from the ground where the person last stood. Except in emergencies where the dog's life or the officer's life is threatened, police dogs inflict no harm.

With its ears perked up, a K-9 listens to its partner.

A tracking team follows a scent.

On the handler's command, the police dog begins a search. When the dog finds the person, it stands guard and barks until the officer arrives. If the suspect fights or threatens the dog, the K-9 will grab hold of his or her arm or leg until the officer arrives.

In one case in San Francisco, California, a ninety-pound yellow-and-black shepherd named Thor responded with his handler to a purse snatching. When the pair arrived on the scene, the victim described the suspect as wearing a white raincoat. She told the officer the man had fled to a nearby wooded area. The officer unsnapped his dog's leash and commanded the dog to begin searching.

Thor covered the lot in wide circles and soon narrowed his search to a dense growth of bushes. Thor stopped and barked furiously, but his partner could not find anything in the thick brush. So Thor dove into the bushes and came out with a large piece of white raincoat. Soon a voice yelled out, "Hold that dog, hold that dog! I'm coming out."[2] With the purse returned and the man booked on suspicion of robbery, Thor received his reward: high praise, a scratch behind his ears, and his usual two dog biscuits.

The ability to flush out crime suspects is matched by the ability to find illegal drugs. Drug-sniffing dogs work with law enforcement officers at border checkpoints, airline terminals, seaports, and even schools to detect the presence of illegal drugs. The K-9s poke around mail

A padded sleeve protects an officer pretending to be a suspect.

A K-9 sniffs for drugs under the seat of a car.

and baggage on conveyor belts, jump on cargo at docks, and even explore vehicles for drugs. A detector dog can accomplish these probing jobs in a fraction of the time it takes a human officer. For example, inspecting a vehicle for drugs takes a detector dog about one minute compared to twenty minutes if done by a person.

People **smuggle** drugs into the United States in clothing, in body cavities, and in luggage. When bags are being loaded onto the luggage carousel outside the airport building, detector dogs leap from one bag to another sniffing for **narcotics**.

In one instance, at John F. Kennedy International Airport in New York, a police dog named Mojo began pawing and biting at a bag being unloaded from an airplane on its way to the baggage claim area. Mojo's behavior signaled that he had detected illegal drugs. So Mojo and his handler followed the bag to the baggage

A working dog sniffs luggage for illegal drugs.

claim area, where they spotted a respectable-looking man in his forties claim it.

A **customs** inspector, whose job is to watch for illegal drugs and other outlawed items entering the country, searched the bag but found nothing unusual in it. Trusting Mojo's skillful scenting abilities, the inspector randomly chose two cans from the toilet articles kit. One bore a label of antiperspirant and the other hair spray. Upon examination, the inspector found them filled with the drug **hashish**. The passenger had drilled holes in the sides of the cans, poured out the contents, filled the cans with hashish, soldered the holes shut, and pasted little price tags over the sealed holes.

Valuable Partners

Police officers who work with dogs tell many stories that show the value of their K-9 partners. Corky, a drug-sniffing cocker spaniel who works at Miami International Airport, proved his worth after only one year on the job. In his first year, Corky sniffed out more than 300 pounds of **marijuana** and over 150 pounds of **cocaine**.

Corky's partner, Officer Ricky Grim, fondly recalls one instance when he and Corky walked by a line of people awaiting customs inspection. When Corky sat down at the feet of a woman standing in the line, it was a signal that he had detected the scent of drugs hidden somewhere on her body. When officers searched the woman, they found vials of liquid cocaine hidden under her clothing. Such successes are all in a day's work for a police dog.

Chapter Two

Why Dogs Are Good for Police Work

A keen sense of smell, sharp eyesight, alert hearing, and the ability to learn many tasks are the qualities that make dogs so valuable to law enforcement. Dogs can smell, see, and hear far better than the average person.

K-9 Senses

For example, a dog can sniff an object touched by a suspect, such as a steering wheel or a car seat, and track his or her scent for several blocks and sometimes even farther. K-9 trainer Bob Eden tells a story about a German shepherd named Lance who once tracked a burglary suspect through a busy city for four miles. The dog finally caught up with the suspect, but only after a route that forced him to jump over some thirty fences.

Dogs can also pick up human scent by sniffing naturally shed skin cells. The average person sheds 50 to 60

U.S. Police Canine Association, Feb., 2001. Alloutdoors.com, Feb., 2001.

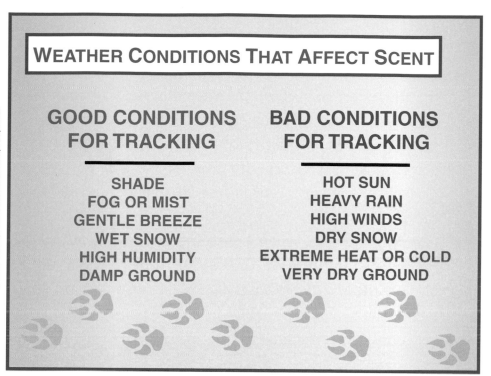

WEATHER CONDITIONS THAT AFFECT SCENT

GOOD CONDITIONS FOR TRACKING	BAD CONDITIONS FOR TRACKING
SHADE	HOT SUN
FOG OR MIST	HEAVY RAIN
GENTLE BREEZE	HIGH WINDS
WET SNOW	DRY SNOW
HIGH HUMIDITY	EXTREME HEAT OR COLD
DAMP GROUND	VERY DRY GROUND

million skin cells each day. These bits of skin settle around a person's feet while walking. Following the invisible trail left by these shed skin cells, one dog can cover as much ground as a hundred people searching for clues to a person's path.

A dog's sense of smell is so sensitive that it can learn to identify some odors and ignore others. Sometimes, people try to disguise illegal drugs by surrounding them with strong-smelling coffee or cinnamon or some other legal substance. A trained drug-sniffing dog can pick out the scent of the illegal drug even when it is disguised by another scent.

"There's no machine on the planet that tops a dog's **olfactory** [smell] system," says Los Angeles police officer

Tim Cooper. "Say you're cooking a pot of vegetable soup. When a human enters the room, he or she takes a whiff and thinks, *Ah, vegetable soup.* End of smell. A dog smells the tomatoes, the celery, the zucchini, the carrots, the oregano, the pepper, your perfume, your deodorant, the natural gas you're using to cook the soup, and the stuff you cleaned the counter with three days ago."[3]

Besides having a sense of smell that is superior to human's, dogs can see greater distances than people can. Most people, when they look straight ahead, can see objects and motion directly in front of them and also on either side of them. Because a dog's eyes are on

Dogs have a very keen sense of smell.

Canine Versus Human Vision

Range of Vision for Dogs with Eyes Facing Forward

Range of Vision for Dogs with Eyes Set to the Side

Range of Human Vision

Hans-J. Ullman, *The New Dog Handbook*, 1985.

the sides of its head, a dog not only sees straight ahead and on either side of where it is standing but also behind it, almost in a complete circle.

Dogs also have sharper vision than do people. A dog can detect movement at up to one hundred yards, which is about the length of a football field. For example, a dog can detect the movement of a mouse at that distance. A person could not. In addition, where humans cannot see in complete darkness, a dog not only sees but can detect movement.

The third important sense of a K-9 is its hearing ability. A dog can hear sounds from several different

Dogs swivel and point their ears toward the direction of sounds.

directions. The dog directs one ear toward one sound and swivels the other ear toward the second sound. Dogs can also hear a wider range of tones than people. For example, certain whistles used for training dogs can be heard by dogs but not by people. This keen sense of hearing played an important role in saving lives during the Vietnam War. Dogs could actually hear wind blowing through trip wires connected to explosives, and warn soldiers of the danger before they stepped into the wires.

K-9 Training

Dogs are not the only animals with a highly developed sense of smell, sight, and hearing. They are one of the few, however, that can also learn many tasks, and learn them quickly. The typical police dog, no matter what its job, must learn to obey commands, track, search, find, and confine.

For instance, during a weekly training session in Anaheim, California, five police dogs participate in a series of drills. One exercise is to find a "decoy suspect" hiding in a building. Upon the command of its partner/handler, the dog leads its partner into the building and in the direction of the hiding **decoy**, or pretend suspect. The dog sniffs its way to track the suspect to a specific room or even upstairs. Then, upon command, it finds and confines the suspect until its partner arrives. This drill combines obeying, tracking, searching, finding, and confining.

Police officers work with their K-9s in obedience training.

K-9 Characteristics

Not all dogs can do police work. Years of experience have shown that certain dogs do better than others. A typical police dog is between one to four years old, male, and weighs forty to fifty pounds. It can be any one of a variety of breeds, including Labrador retrievers, golden retrievers, Belgian Malinois, and, depending on the job, beagles and cocker spaniels, too.

The breed most often used for police work, however, is the German shepherd. Almost three-fourths of police dogs are German shepherds. Police favor this breed over other breeds because they are intelligent, capable of aggression, and possess an exceptionally good sense of smell. Loyalty, alertness, and **stamina** are other traits that make this breed a good choice for police work. What's more, the German shepherd is matchless in its ability to recognize airborne scents and follow scents on the ground.

Protecting Their Partners

No matter what the breed, the mark of a good police dog is a high level of alertness, obedience, and protectiveness of its partner. A police dog will only bite under three conditions: when ordered by its partner; when it senses someone is threatening its partner; or when it feels endangered itself. In these cases, the K-9 bites to control the suspect. If a police officer is being threatened, he or she must be able to rely on the dog to bite

Use of Police Dogs by Breed

71%   9%   2%   1%

12%   2%   2%   1%

German   Labrador   Bloodhound   Doberman
Shepherd   Retriever   Pinscher

Belgian   Golden   Rottweiler   All other
Malinois   Retriever   breeds

Percentage of use by breed
Information supplied by the North American Police Work Dog Association.

K-9 Baron practices apprehending skills with police officer Mark Brucks.

on command. In some cases, a dog will even come between a shooting suspect and its partner in order to protect the officer.

It is also essential that a police dog not be easily distracted by loud noises, such as gunfire, in risky situations. Some dangerous jobs that police dogs encounter include chasing and **apprehending** an armed suspect, sniffing for hidden bombs, and searching through earthquake rubble for buried victims. A dog that is smart, faithful, strong, and brave is likely to be a good police dog.

Chapter Three

Training

Most police dogs and their handlers undergo at least ten to fourteen weeks of training. During that time, a dog must learn obedience, tracking, searching, finding, holding, and in some cases detection. Above all, the dog must learn to obey and protect its human partner.

The key to all police dog training is the reward system. Beginning in training, the handler rewards the dog often with praise, such as "Good dog" or "Great job." Affectionate hand contact, such as a hug or rub behind the ears and head are also rewards. Sometimes the handler will play tug-of-war or a round of ball throwing with the dog. Rewards such as these help form a bond between the dog and its handler. When a strong bond develops, the dog becomes eager to please its partner.

At the start of training, dogs are assigned a partner, or handler. Usually the dog is paired with this officer for its entire length of service, a period that may last as many as five or six years.

An officer rewards her K-9 partner for a job well done.

The first stage of training is much like obedience training for any dog. The dog learns both voice commands and hand signals for heel, sit, stay, down, and come. Once a dog has mastered these simple commands, training moves ahead.

Because police dogs might have to jump over barricades and through open windows, squirm under fences, snake through barbed wire, scale wet slippery rocks, and balance on logs, they must undergo **agility** training. The dogs work on a variety of drills to prepare them for any rugged or hazardous groundwork they may encounter on the job. During agility training, the dogs climb ladders, zigzag across junk piles, and coast down playground slides.

As the K-9 training progresses, handlers add new commands and skills. At the "find" command, the unleashed dog locates and corners a suspect by barking and guarding until the partner arrives. In practice, another officer acts as a suspect, or decoy, and hides inside a vacant building.

The handler and K-9 (muzzled during training to prevent bites) search for the decoy. The officer first warns the hiding suspect, saying that he has a trained

A police dog climbs a ladder during agility training.

dog. The suspect is told to come out or the dog will come in. Usually the suspect comes out when he or she hears about the dog. Dogs are taught to take a "sit" or "down" position when the officer handcuffs a suspect.

Another command the dog must learn is "track." A tracking situation occurs when the handler possesses an article that has the scent of either a lost person or a crime suspect. The dog sniffs the article and the handler commands the dog to track. When tracking, the K-9 wears a harness and tracking **lead**, or leash, held by the handler. The K-9 is following a ground or airborne scent. On a thirty-foot leash, the sniffing dog may weave in a wide back-and-forth pattern.

An officer handcuffs a suspect while his K-9 takes a "down" position.

An excited K-9 on a lead tracks a scent.

Drug Detection

Depending on the job a dog is going to do, there may be additional training. For example, drug detector teams require four to six extra weeks of training. During that time the dog must learn to detect the scents of commonly smuggled drugs such as marijuana, cocaine, **heroin**, and **methamphetamine**.

The training begins through play. Two-year-old Hunter, a yellow Labrador, and his handler, Joe, play tug-of-war with a rolled-up towel. In no time at all, the towel becomes Hunter's favorite toy. It will also serve as a key tool in Hunter's training.

Once Hunter forms an attachment to the rolled-up towel, Joe places marijuana inside of it. Hunter has to find and **retrieve** this "play object." Joe hides the towel in various indoor and outdoor locations. When Hunter finds the towel, Joe praises and plays with him. Hunter learns to associate the scent of the drugs with his beloved towel.

After a while, Joe hides the drugs without the towel. Joe commands Hunter to find the drugs. Hunter excitedly obeys. Each time Hunter finds the hidden drugs, Joe brings out the towel for a game of tug-of-war. After six weeks, Hunter is an expert at finding anything with the odor of marijuana on it. Joe uses the same method for training Hunter in detecting the unique scents of other drugs.

Once a dog learns to detect the scent of the drugs, it must also learn how to alert the officer. The dogs learn

Sniffing luggage for drugs is part of a drug detector's job.

A dog that finds illegal drugs will give a signal.

two types of signals. One is a passive alert, where the K-9 just sits next to the detected odor. The other is an aggressive alert, where the dog jumps onto luggage or crates and paws at the container.

As part of the training, the handler hides narcotics in a crate or some other container commonly used by drug smugglers. During one such training session, Hunter finds a carton, pulls it away from the others, and gives aggressive alerts, such as pawing or biting on the container. For his efforts, Hunter receives praise from his handler and is rewarded with a quick game of tug-of-war with his towel.

Bomb Detection

Dogs that will work on bomb detection squads undergo similar training except they must learn to identify the odor of explosives. Before mastering this skill, dogs endure weeks of "nose time." They are able to sniff only a few hours a day before they tire. It takes six to eight weeks before the dogs learn to recognize up to seventeen different scents of explosives ranging from gunpowder to dynamite.

Working with a customs agent, a dog searches for drugs.

A bomb detector dog watches its handler check for explosives.

One training method uses an eight-inch piece of plastic pipe with tiny holes in it. The trainer puts one type of explosive inside the pipe. Caps on each end seal the material inside, leaving the scent to escape through the small holes. The trainer lets the dog sniff the filled pipe and then hides it in a variety of places proceeding from easy to more difficult. For example, the trainer first sets the pipe on flat ground and waits for the dog to find it. Next, he hides the pipe in tall grass. Next, he conceals the pipe in boxes, vehicles, trees, buildings, and sometimes even buries it to see if the dog can locate the pipe.

Due to the delicate nature of explosives, dogs are trained to give only passive alerts, such as sitting next to the substance. Once a dog shows that it recognizes the odor of each explosive, it undergoes a final test. The handler places six boxes before the dog. The dog must successfully find the correct box with an explosive and sit next to it.

A plastic training pipe has holes in it to allow the scent to seep out.

Testing

To qualify for K-9 duty, teams must pass a battery of tests. They must locate a person hiding in an open field by air scent, track a person off the trail and in the brush, find people hidden in three different places, and conduct a night search. Trainers certify teams that successfully complete all exercises for obedience, tracking and trailing, evidence retrieval, and building search. Certification means that the teams have finished their formal K-9 training and are ready for patrol work.

Chapter Four

Off Duty

The special relationship between an officer and his or her K-9 partner continues even when the workday—and the dog's police career—ends. After hours, the dog goes home with its partner. Usually it takes on the role of family dog. As a family pet, the K-9 romps alongside kids on their bicycles. Some K-9s even go on family vacations. For some dogs the transition from police work to family dog and back to police work is relatively easy.

One K-9, a Bouvier named Farns, worked for fourteen months for the Irvine, California, police department. The huge 120-pound dog was fearless at his police duties. Off duty, however, Farns was as gentle as could be. His partner's wife ran a day-care service for preschoolers. Farns let the children tug at his ears and thick wiry fur without a whimper of protest. Sometimes the couple's three-year-old son slept on a rug with his head between Farns's great bearlike paws. But at work, Farns was all business. "His personality changed the minute I put on his working collar,"[4] said his partner, Officer Steve Frew.

Farns, a Bouvier like this dog, was an outstanding police dog and a gentle family pet.

For other K-9s, there is no transition to being a family pet while a working dog. For example, a bomb detector dog needs to strongly focus on its job and therefore cannot be a pet. Because a bomb detector dog's average day is uneventful, it must have a high point in its life and that is its job. The dog must be eager to work and to earn a reward. The dog's only reward is to chase a pitched ball, play a game of tug-of-war, or gulp down a treat when it finds an explosive.

If the bomb detector dog gets to play off duty, it will not do its job. Therefore, a bomb detector dog lives in kennels only. It travels from the kennel at its partner's house to the kennel at the bomb squad station. When the dog is taken out to do a job, it knows it is not to play, but to work.

Off-Duty K-9s

Most police dogs work twelve-hour shifts, three days a week. The job can be strenuous. Mentally they learn to obey dozens of commands. Physically they can be expected to climb ladders, sprint at speeds up to forty miles per hour in pursuit of criminals, sniff out narcotics and evidence, track and corner fleeing suspects,

Over 70 percent of K-9s are German shepherds.

and defend their partner from attackers. For these reasons, off-duty K-9s are expected to rest. Like their human partners, they can tire from too much work. But even in their off-duty time, the officer and dog must practice daily to keep their skills sharp. Depending on the dog's job, the K-9 will be drilled in obedience, agility, and "find" exercises.

For example, Officer Danny Miller races his German shepherd Olden around his Altus, Oklahoma, backyard each day to build up his stamina. To test Olden's obedience, Officer Miller gives his K-9 the "stay" command and then goes for a walk. A half hour later, Olden is still glued to the spot where Officer

Agility training includes high jumps.

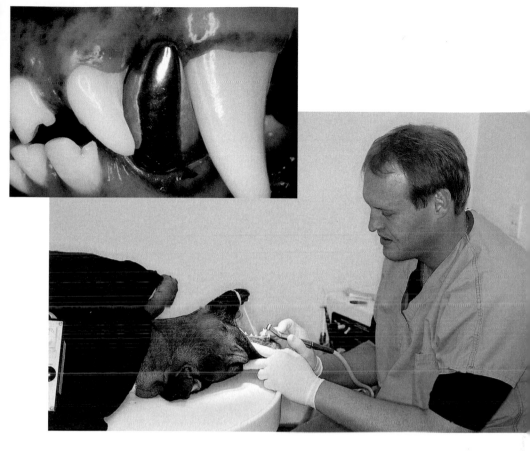

A K-9 gets a new silver crown over a cracked tooth.

Miller left him. Officer Miller gives Olden praise and a good scratch behind the ears. These drills keep the K-9 physically and mentally fit.

Retirement

Although some K-9s work until age ten or eleven, most retire after age eight. By that time, they can no longer perform the strenuous work that is required of them as patrol dogs. When a dog retires, it usually becomes a family pet for its partner. Nearly all police officers keep their K-9 partners. In rare cases, when an officer does not keep the dog, the dog would be given to another officer, a relative, or sometimes back to the breeder. This might occur when an officer gets a new K-9, and the older dog dominates or clashes with the new dog.

When Police Constable Bob Eden's K-9 Lance became too old to serve, he trained a second K-9 named Stryker. Lance came into the house to live and Stryker lived in the backyard kennel.

Sometimes the hardest part of retirement for the dog is getting used to *not* going to work with his partner. Officer Andy Jimenez retired his K-9 Falco at age eight. Falco was only allowed to spend ten minutes a

A K-9's off-duty job includes visits to schools.

Officer Andy Jimenez and his K-9 partner Falco were a team for eight years.

day in the house, otherwise he lived in his outdoor kennel, where he felt safe and secure. It took Falco about a month to get used to the idea that he could no longer go in the squad car with Officer Jimenez. As Falco saw Officer Jimenez in uniform leaving for his job, the K-9 jumped up, barked, and howled when he could not join his partner.

Valued Workers

K-9s, with their keen senses of smell, eyesight, and hearing have shown over and over their value in law

A strong bond forms between an officer and his or her K-9 partner.

enforcement. In some types of work, detection, for example, they routinely outperform humans. A trained dog team can often root out suspects and hidden drugs more quickly than an officer working alone. There is one added benefit. Dogs can do this work without violence. "You can't call back a bullet," one police chief says. "You *can* call back a dog."[5]

City after city has had success with K-9 teams. More successes will likely follow as a result of the hard work and dedication of trainers, officers, and the dogs themselves.

Notes

1. Interview with Andy Jimenez, police officer and K-9 trainer, Anaheim, California, December 2000.

2. Quoted in Clarke Newlon, *Police Dogs in Action.* New York: Dodd, Mead, 1974, p. 51.

3. Quoted in Karen Karbo, "Stopping to Smell the Luggage," *Avenues,* November/December 1997, p. 24.

4. Quoted in Emily and Per Ola d'Aulaire, "I'm Going to Miss You, Farns," *Reader's Digest,* June 1985, pp. 67–68.

5. Quoted in d'Aulaire, "I'm Going to Miss You, Farns," p. 66.

Glossary

agility: The ability to move quickly and easily.

apprehend: To arrest.

cocaine: A narcotic, sometimes called crack, that looks like white pebbles or sand.

customs: Duties or monetary payments, paid to the government, imposed on items brought in from other countries.

decoy: A "pretend" suspect or criminal.

drug: An illegal narcotic substance that dulls the senses.

explosive: A substance, especially a prepared chemical, that explodes suddenly.

hashish: A narcotic extract prepared from the dried flowers of the hemp plant.

heroin: An illegal, highly addictive, and dangerous drug made from the seed pod of certain varieties of poppy plants.

lead: A leash, or restrictive band, to lead an animal.

marijuana: Dried and shredded flower clusters and leaves of the hemp plant that are smoked for stimulation or a drunken effect.

methamphetamine: A white, odorless, and bitter-tasting crystalline powder.

narcotic: A drug that dulls the senses, induces sleep, and becomes addictive with prolonged use.

olfactory: Relating to the sense of smell.

retrieve: To find and bring back.

search: To explore thoroughly in order to find an object or a person.

smuggle: To illegally bring something in or out of a country.

stamina: The physical ability to do something for a long time.

suspect: A person believed to have committed a crime.

track: To follow the footprints or traces of a lost or hidden person.

Organizations to Contact

Canine Detector Services, Inc.
34 Tuckahoe Road, Suite 340
Marmora, NJ 08223
(609) 442-1111
www.k9detector.com
The website describes this private company's services to schools for detecting drugs and firearms on campuses. Dogs can detect gunpowder, shotgun shells and bullets, handguns, and other explosives.

Canine Intercept School Programs
3525 North Causeway Boulevard, Suite 607
Metairie, LA 70002
(888) 404-SNIF
www.canineintercept.com
The website describes confidential programs for schools.

Falco K9 Academy
3920 Prospect Avenue, Unit C
Yorba Linda, CA 92686
(909) 522-7806
www.falcok9academy.com
The website describes the academy's mission of team training of K-9s and their handlers. The goal of owner

and trainer Officer Andy Jimenez is to meet the unique needs of law enforcement.

Police Dog Home Page
Eden & Ney Associates, Inc.
12894–63A Avenue
Surrey, British Columbia, Canada
V3X 1S5
(800) 955-2962
www.policek9.com
The website lists K-9–related books and articles, handler and dog performance standards, police officers and dogs killed in service, and shows photos of Constable Bob Eden's dogs, Lance and Stryker.

For Further Exploration

Charles and Linda George, *Patrol Dogs.* New York: River-Front Books, 1998. Describes the best breeds for patrol dogs as well as basic and advanced training of the dogs.

M. L. Papurt, *Compatible Canines.* Hauppauge, NY: Barron's, 1999. Information for readers on how to train a dog. Topics include basic commands, equipment, behavior, and teaching a dog to relate to other animals within the household.

Lisa Rosenthal, *A Dog's Best Friend.* Chicago: Chicago Review Press, 1999. Over fifty activities and crafts teach young children how to take care of their dogs while developing a bonding friendship.

Charlotte Wilcox, *The German Shepherd.* Mankato, MN: Capstone Press, 1996. An introduction to the intelligent, fearless German shepherd dog. Includes the dog's history, development, uses, and care.

Index

Picture Credits

About the Author

Judith Janda Presnall is an award-winning nonfiction writer. Her books include *Rachel Carson, Artificial Organs, The Giant Panda, Oprah Winfrey, Mount Rushmore, Life on Alcatraz, Animals That Glow, Animal Skeletons,* and *Circuses.* Presnall graduated from the University of Wisconsin in Whitewater. She is a recipient of the Jack London Award for meritorious service in the California Writers Club. She is also a member of the Society of Children's Book Writers and Illustrators. She lives in the Los Angeles area with her husband Lance.